A MOMENT IN TIME WITH

ALBERTOSAURUS

Eric P. Felber, Philip J. Currie
and Jan Sovak

TROODON
PRODUCTIONS INC

Acknowledgement

Only three names appear on the cover as authors and illustrator. However, many other people helped get this book to print. We'd like to say a special thank you to our families who patiently listened to our endless ideas; some of them good, and some of them bad. We'd like to thank Karen Kryschuk for her help in organising this book. Her efforts made all of our jobs easier.

To all others who helped, thank you very much.

Eric P. Felber, Philip J. Currie and Jan Sovak

A MOMENT IN TIME* WITH ALBERTOSAURUS

*trade-mark of Troodon Productions Inc.

Text by Eric P. Felber and Philip J. Currie
Illustrations by Jan Sovak
Edited by Laura Purdy Editing Services

COPYRIGHT ©1998 TROODON PRODUCTIONS INC.

"A MOMENT IN TIME" BOOKS ARE PUBLISHED BY
TROODON PRODUCTIONS INC., Suite 1910, 355 4th Avenue S.W.
Calgary, Alberta T2P OJ1, Canada

CREDITS

Design and cover by Aventinum, Prague
Colour separation and typesetting by Baroa, Prague
Printed and bound by Polygrafia , Prague
6/02/76/51-01

CANADIAN CATALOGUING IN PUBLICATION DATA

Felber, Eric P. (Eric Peter), 1960-
A moment in time with Albertosaurus

1. Albertosaurus - Juvenile fiction. I. Currie, Philip
J., 1949- II.Sovak, Jan, 1953- III. Title.

ISBN 0-9682512-1-8

PS8561.E42M63 1998   jC813'.54   C98-900202-0

PR9199.3.F43M63 1998

PREFACE

Try to imagine the power and ferocity of a single three tonne carnivorous dinosaur. Then, imagine nine or ten of these beasts living and hunting together as a pack. This frightening thought was reality for many herbivores that lived alongside the mighty members of the tyrannosaur family. This book is about **Albertosaurus**, the tyrannosaur family member whose fossilised remains we have had the most opportunity to study.

In 1910, Barnum Brown of the American Museum of Natural History (New York) discovered a bone bed along the Red Deer River in Alberta, Canada. Not until 1996 was the full significance of this discovery realised. Currently the bones of nine **Albertosaurus** have been uncovered. This has provided the first real evidence of packing behaviour among large carnivorous dinosaurs. This bone bed also makes us question what catastrophic event caused at least nine of these amazing animals to die at the same time.

Numerous other fossil sites in Alberta paint a picture of dinosaur life in the late Cretaceous period. It was information from these fossil sites that enabled us to write this book. The story, even though a work of fiction, uses the actual scientific information known about **Albertosaurus**. These facts are presented at the end of the story.

A **Moment In Time With Albertosaurus** is the second book in a series of stories. The series will focus on the scientific facts known about specific prehistoric animals. This information will bring a moment in time to life for you.

ALBERTOSAURUS

Fog shrouded the majesty of the late *Cretaceous* landscape. The horizon sparkled as the rays of early dawn glistened on the forest canopy. Many species of *herbivores* were beginning their daily search for food. Their bellows and grunts punctuated the morning. The fog melted into the atmosphere as a group of *ankylosaurs* appeared one by one in a small clearing of the forest.

This morning, as usual, the forest was a noisy place. The ankylosaurs began their *foraging.* Lush vegetation in the small clearing provided a generous source of food. The armour plated ankylosaurs gorged on the ferns and *cycads* around them.

Suddenly, the noisy forest fell silent. One of the older ankylosaurs lifted his head, aware of the sinister silence that surrounded his family group. The old animal could see movement in a tall stand of *conifers* not too far away. Turning his head quickly, he could see more movement to his right. He shifted his great mass with unexpected speed, and swung the bony club on the end of his tail, smashing it into a tree trunk. The resounding thunk alerted the rest of the herd to danger.

From behind the cover of the forest a huge *Albertosaurus* leapt out and ran toward the ankylosaurs. From all sides of the clearing, nine more *tyrannosaurs* emerged, each letting out thunderous roars as they approached the *agitated* herd of ankylosaurs. By now the ankylosaurs gathered into a loose group in the centre of the clearing. The adults formed a defensive circle, all animals facing inward, with their tails toward the predators. The young intuitively moved toward the protective centre of the circle. The wide spacing of the adults seemed to leave the young open to attack, but the defenders

needed room to swing their tails back and forth. The mass of bone at the end of an ankylosaur's tail was an awkward yet formidable weapon.

The *Albertosaurus* knew well the damage that those impressive tails could do. Circling the ankylosaurs cautiously, the hunters snapped their jaws and jerked their heads forward with intimidating gestures.

As they watched the movements of the predators, the ankylosaurs shifted their huge bodies from one foot to the other, their tails swinging in great slow moving arcs. The ear shattering roars and the snapping jaws of the *Albertosaurus* were meant to intimidate and confuse the prey, but these ankylosaurs temporarily felt secure in their defensive circle. A stand-off ensued.

The adults held their formation, and watched the giant flesh eaters. Many of the ankylosaurs bore the scars of previous encounters and were not going to be caught unaware.

Losing patience, some of the older tyrannosaurs gave up and started to move towards the edge of the clearing. But suddenly a young *Albertosaurus*, who had been pacing persistently around the herbivores, let out a terrific roar and charged through an opening between two of the adult ankylosaurs. Perhaps he was driven by hunger, or perhaps he was simply overconfident in the agility and speed of his long legs and lightly built body. With eyes focused on the cluster of unarmoured young, he lowered his head to strike at the closest juvenile. Without warning, a bony tail club from one of the adults grazed the side of his face. It was a glancing blow, but it snapped three of his teeth and opened a gaping wound above his mouth. He was lucky to escape with such a mild injury. If he had received the full force of the ankylosaur's tail, he would have dropped in his tracks. He retreated from the circle before the ankylosaur had a chance to strike again

As soon as he was out of danger, the young tyrannosaur turned. Maddened by pain and the taste of his own blood seeping through smashed teeth, he charged again. The infuriated tyrannosaur had learned nothing from his first experience, and he raced once more for the wide opening between the adults. One of the old, experienced ankylosaurs was ready this time. Pushing hard with his front legs, the front of his body swung away from the *predator* with a speed that was unbelievable for his great bulk. With his hind legs flexed slightly at the knees, he had been swinging his hips back and forth, building momentum. The machine was in motion, and nothing could stop it now. The great bony club on the end of the stiff tail swung into view. It was moving fast, and accelerating.

Too late the *Albertosaurus* realised his *peril.* He leapt into the air attempting to get out of the way, but the massive knob of bone caught his left leg, and swept his feet out from underneath him. The *Albertosaurus* came crashing to the ground, cracking four of his ribs on impact. He frantically scrambled to his feet and staggered out of range, stumbling in a red mist of pain and confusion. The smaller of the two bones in his lower leg had been fractured by the ankylosaur's club, and one of the jagged broken ribs had been pushed deep into his abdomen, puncturing his right lung.

Chaos erupted in the centre of the clearing. When the old ankylosaur had swung around to smash the young tyrannosaur, the circle was broken. Before he could regain his position, one of the *Albertosaurus* spotted the opportunity to strike and moved in. The gap closed, but not before the predator had made his way into the centre of the circle. He moved toward one of the smaller ankylosaurs, who instinctively dropped onto her knees. The tail lashed out, but to no effect. Young ankylosaurs had no tail clubs, and had only two rows of armour on the neck for protection. These were effective against raptors, but were useless when the gigantic jaws of the *Albertosaurus* closed on her neck and shoulders. Driven by powerful muscles, the four-inch *serrated* teeth easily penetrated her leathery, bone-studded skin. With a sickening crunch they drove through the bones. The powerful, massive jaws gave the ankylosaur a quick and painless death.

While the *Albertosaurus* attacked the young ankylosaur, the other young herbivores moved away from their fallen comrade. The circle broke and the adults moved off to join the young at the edge of the clearing. The confrontation was over, and both species knew it. The ankylosaurs moved slowly into the forest. They kept a wary eye on the pack of hunters, but for the survivors, life was already returning to normal.

The remaining predators moved towards the kill. Soon the largest individuals were biting and tearing off huge chunks of meat and bone. Growling and snapping at each other, the younger animals waited their turn. The injured *Albertosaurus* painfully dragged himself to the *carcass*. His hunger overcame the pain in his chest and leg. By the time he arrived, most of the flesh had been devoured. The other pack members stepped aside, their appetites largely satisfied. It had been a messy feast but there were enough tidbits left for the late-comer.

Mid-day temperatures rose, and the pack settled down to rest. They would let their tasty meal digest before moving on.

The wounded *Albertosaurus* tried to rest with the others, but he was having more and more difficulty breathing. Blood was slowly filling his lung and abdomen through the hole torn

open by the broken rib. His leg was very swollen and excruciatingly painful. It was impossible for the injured animal to crouch down on his haunches to rest. He stood among the pack, most of whom were stretched out on their bellies with their legs tucked up beneath them. His uninjured leg bore most of his weight. Every time he shifted his bulk, the dull throbbing in the injured leg erupted into a searing bolt of pain.

A few yards away, the remainder of the ankylosaur carcass was being picked over by raptors. Savage predators in their own right, they had been drawn by the scent of fresh blood, and were not above taking advantage of a free meal. From time to time, birds swooped down from the trees to snatch tidbits too small for their larger cousins to notice.

As the afternoon started to cool, the *Albertosaurus* pack rose and moved into the forest. They had no particular destination. They simply followed the *matriarch,* a large, thirty year old female, who had led them on many successful hunts. Her body was heavily scarred from aggressive prey that hadn't died quietly, and from encounters with rival packs of tyrannosaurs. Some injuries had even been received during fights for dominance within her own pack, and from over-zealous suitors. But today, each animal knew where it stood in the pecking order, and this awesome group moved with an uncanny sense of organisation.

Following, but getting ever farther behind, was the wounded *Albertosaurus.* Other days, he had been the fastest individual in the pack. Now he could only walk half his normal speed. His injured leg caused great pain, but it was his difficulty breathing that forced him to stop often. Whenever he got too far behind, the next *Albertosaurus* in line would fall back to keep him in sight. And when that one fell behind the others, the next one in line slowed down too. Eventually the whole pack had reduced its speed. By now they were spread out in a line where no animal could see more than two of the others.

Alone, the chances of survival for an injured animal were poor. But over millions of years, selection had favoured those species which protected their injured pack members. *Albertosaurus* was among those animals that had learned to depend on the security of a group. It was one of the most sophisticated predators the world had yet seen and had surprisingly complex behaviour. The pack depended on these complex behavioural patterns because at some point in their lives, each one of them would be injured. Undoubtedly, the violent lifestyle of a top predator had a high degree of risk. Consequently, each *Albertosaurus* would be forced to rely on the group for help at some time.

At a point where the game trail crossed a stream, the pack stopped to quench their thirst. A small group of *Saurornitholestes* stopped drinking when the first tyrannosaur appeared. Quickly, the smaller creatures disappeared into the cover of the forest. Weighing less than a human, they did not want to encounter their much larger cousins. These sleek animals were agile and fast, but they sometimes learned the hard way that the young tyrannosaurs were even faster. Fortunately for them, even the smallest *Albertosaurus* in this pack had grown too large to find them of interest.

Once in hiding, the small *carnivores* watched, waiting for the *Albertosaurus* pack to move on so they could continue their daily routine. Then, a gentle breeze blowing down the game trail carried the unmistakable scent of blood to their keen nostrils. Peering from behind the cover of leaves, their eyes opened wide to fix on the wounded *Albertosaurus* who limped into view, clotted blood on his face and leg.

Oblivious to the presence of the raptors, the rest of the tyrannosaurs moved into the more open *parkland* west of the stream. When the injured male crossed the stream, the *Saurornitholestes* moved out from their forest hideout and followed him at a distance. They could see that he was too weak to chase them.

Within a short time after crossing the stream, the wounded giant fell farther behind the group. His breathing was laboured with his punctured lung working at less than half efficiency. The loss of blood and the excruciating pain blurred his vision. He could no longer see his companions up ahead. His senses were dulled to the point that he was not even aware of the danger following close behind. The six *Saurornitholestes* would not attack as long as he was on his feet, but they could sense that he might not be standing for long.

The young tyrannosaur stumbled. Although he tried to regain his balance, his foot slipped and he came down hard, rolling onto his back to protect his injured ribs. Thinking that their chance had come, one of the bolder *Saurornitholestes* rushed toward the fallen beast and leapt onto the side of the *Albertosaurus.* As the long sickle claws of the *Saurornitholestes* ripped into his skin, the *Albertosaurus* let out a high pitched shriek of pain and anger.

A second *Saurornitholestes* followed the lead attacker by only a few seconds. He latched onto the back of the wounded beast's leg, his claws tearing through skin and muscle. Too late he realised that the *Albertosaurus* was far from finished. The great jaws came around with blinding speed and snapped shut on the tormentor, cutting him completely in half. The first

attacker was thrown across the path as the giant rolled over and pulled himself to his feet in one motion.

The *Albertosaurus* pack spun around as soon as they heard the shriek from their comrade. Two of the youngest, lightest animals were immediately on their way back. By this time, the remaining *Saurornitholestes* were defending themselves against the wounded male. The tyrannosaur had forgotten his pain in an *adrenaline* rage. He charged the closest raptors. The smaller animals were more agile, however, and easily evaded his rush. One of the *Saurornitholestes* launched himself onto the side of the giant as he charged by. When the *Albertosaurus* felt the claws dig into his flesh, he threw himself to the ground so rapidly that the raptor did not have time to disengage his claws. The smaller animal was crushed under two tonnes of falling *Albertosaurus.* A blood-curdling roar froze the remaining raptors. They looked up to see the reinforcements arriving and scattered into the underbrush. They were pursued for only a short distance by the less manoeuvrable tyrannosaurs.

By the time the two young *Albertosaurus* returned to their wounded comrade, the rest of the pack was waiting for them. The young male was still on the ground where he last fell, and was visibly gulping for air. His exertions had taken a toll, but something greater was causing his gasping. When he fell on the *Saurornitholestes,* the impact had driven the broken rib deeper into his body and was now causing massive internal bleeding. One by one, the pack lay down to rest near their comrade. It was only a matter of time now before the great beast died from his injuries. Occasionally, the resting protectors looked at the injured animal but there was nothing more to be done.

Before long, the *Saurornitholestes* came quietly back, and crouched behind trees and bushes. They watched and waited. The large eyes of the small carnivores still stared at the protective circle as nightfall engulfed the beautiful late Cretaceous landscape.

Sometime during the night, the young male *Albertosaurus* succumbed to his wounds. Before dawn, the matriarch rose and nuzzled the carcass, as if to check for signs of life. The glassy eyes did not flicker but stared lifelessly at the bushes where the raptors lay in hiding. The other tyrannosaurs were soon on their feet. As the first rays of sunlight caught the treetops, the nine surviving *Albertosaurus* moved off to the west.

When the last tyrannosaur disappeared around a corner in the trail, four *Saurornitholestes* broke cover and hesitantly approached the body stretched out next to the path. Sure at last of the giant's *demise,* one raptor let out a hideous shriek and leaped onto the carcass. Not far down the path, the matriarch heard and understood. There would be no going back this time.

Hours later, the pack emerged from the open parkland onto the edge of a wide, treeless plain. Predators, including other *Albertosaurus* packs, were somewhere on the open plain too. The group was wary of impending danger from rival carnivores as they passed the last stand of trees.

They paused to sniff the air, trying to pick up the scent of potential prey in the vicinity. With their heads held high, some snorted when they did not find any enticing odours. *Albertosaurus* relied as heavily on scent as it did on eyesight.

The pack knew that this was the time of year when many species of duck-bills and *ceratopsians* were collecting into great herds for their northern migration. The preferred diet of *Albertosaurus* was *hadrosaur.* This duck-billed herbivore's bulky size and armourless body made it easy prey if it could be caught away from its herd. The great hunters pressed out onto the open plain.

Soon they came upon fresh tracks on a well-trampled trail. The trail was many body lengths across and was dotted with dung piles. This was the *migratory* path of the herds. It was obvious to the *Albertosaurus* that a herd of hadrosaurs had passed this way not long before. Instinct turned their steps north.

As the summer wore on and the sun mounted higher, this area would become unbearably hot. Not only was it cooler far to the north, but the vegetation was perfect for fattening up young herbivores. Twenty-four hours of sunshine each summer day produced rapid and lush plant growth which was much more nutritious than vegetation in lower latitudes.

The pack moved at a leisurely pace for several hours. Even so, it was inevitable that they would eventually catch up with the hadrosaur herd. They were sleeker, faster animals than the hadrosaurs and they did not need to stop as often to feed. As the sun climbed, the scent of the great herbivores became stronger. The hungry predators increased their pace.

A shrieking noise ahead signaled the presence of a group of flying reptiles. Four large *Quetzalcoatlus* were feeding on the carcass of a young hadrosaur. A group of raptors stood off to one side, looking for opportunities to rush in and steal a tidbit or two. The raptors had a healthy respect for the long, sharp beaks of *Quetzalcoatlus.* They waited impatiently for their chance. *Albertosaurus* however, was large and powerful and paid little attention to the flying reptiles. The nine big predators moved within sight of the carcass. The raptors watched the tyrannosaurs arrive and decided there was no point in waiting for tidbits now. They turned and disappeared into the ferns and cycads.

The flying reptiles became aware of the approaching *Albertosaurus* and took up defensive positions. Opening up their impressive wing spans in an attempt to look larger and more aggressive, they emitted deafening, high-pitched squeals. These tactics worked on the younger members of the *Albertosaurus* pack. They stopped to stare transfixed at the noisy creatures in front of them. However, the older adults in the pack had encountered the flying reptiles before. They were familiar with these intimidating gestures and were not afraid.

The beaks of the *Quetzalcoatlus* were razor sharp weapons which demanded a certain amount of respect. They may have been able to hold one or two of the huge carnivores at bay. However, they did not stand much chance against nine.

The young *Albertosaurus* sensed that the older pack members did not fear the *Quetzalcoatlus*. They quickly overcame their own hesitation and joined the advance. Together, the tyrannosaurs approached the defenders, snapping their jaws and fanning out to surround the flying reptiles.

When the *Quetzalcoatlus* saw the huge creatures snapping at them from all sides, they knew they had lost. The giant reptiles spread their wings and flapped in long smooth strokes. Slowly each lifted off the ground, stirring up a tremendous amount of dust. Once in the air, they circled over the heads of the *Albertosaurus,* still hoping for a chance to resume their meal. The *Quetzalcoatlus* had consumed most of the flesh before being chased away. The *Albertosaurus*

devoured the remains. Within minutes, only bone fragments and small scraps were left on the ground.

The pack resumed their trek north. On the western horizon, large hills were visible. In a few million years, the rocks beneath their feet would be thrust up into the Rocky Mountains. For now, the pack sensed that the migrating herds were moving parallel to the line of hills. They followed the scent of fresh hadrosaur dung which hung heavy in the air. They knew the herd was close and they hurried their pace.

Later in the day, a strong wind blew in from the north. The *Albertosaurus* could detect the unmistakable scent of their favorite prey, hadrosaur. The herbivores would have been within sight of the *Albertosaurus* pack, except for the fact that the paths wove in and out of heavily matted ferns and cycads. The winding trail obscured a clear view of the herd.

Within an hour, the scent of the herd was overwhelming. The *Albertosaurus* reached the top of a small knoll and came to a full stop. Ahead of them, the trail narrowed between two tree covered slopes. Through this passageway, five to six hundred hadrosaurs moved at a leisurely pace.

The massive predators prepared for the hunt. There was an amazing sense of organisation. The adult females were larger than the males and led the hunt. The younger members of the pack would be responsible for the chase because of their speed and agility. The older *Albertosaurus* would trap and bring down the prey. Four young adults and the matriarch waited impatiently while the other members of the pack moved to a small stand of trees downwind of the herbivore herd. The advance group of tyrannosaurs entered the woods and circled, undetected, ahead of the herd of hadrosaurs.

After waiting an agonising length of time, the female issued a low growl and the rest of the pack made their way slowly down the knoll. They wanted to get as close as possible to the herd before they were seen.

They had not gone far, however, before they were spotted by the herd. The hadrosaurs began bellowing frantically. The ground shook as the three tonne animals ran from the predators behind them. Within moments, the herd was stampeding with the predators in hot pursuit.

The *Albertosaurus* knew that when the herd was in full motion, it would be easier to pick out an old or wounded animal who could not keep up with the rest. The predators closed the gap quickly and raced alongside the herd, snapping their jaws. The female *Albertosaurus* spotted an older animal dropping back from its position in the middle of the herd. She pushed into the stampeding herd attempting to separate the old hadrosaur. The younger predators saw her move and they also focused on the one animal. The key was to remove him from the protection of the herd. The lead *Albertosaurus* managed to manoeuvre herself between the centre of the herd and her chosen victim. The four younger tyrannosaurs were running on the opposite side of the prey. The remaining hadrosaurs angled away from the danger, leaving the one animal singled out.

In a last ditch effort, the old hadrosaur, now separated from the rest, put out a final burst of speed. The young *Albertosaurus* were not yet close enough to catch the hadrosaur. The female tyrannosaur allowed the hadrosaur to continue moving towards the trees. The desperate hadrosaur began to out-distance his pursuers. But as he glanced over his shoulder at the *Albertosaurus* behind, the advance party of *Albertosaurus* crashed out from the trees directly in front of him.

The young carnivores behind slowed their pace to let the experienced adults direct and control the hunt.

On seeing the danger in front, the hadrosaur frantically tried to pass between two of the females. He collided with one of the attackers, but managed to avoid her great jaws. Because the *Albertosaurus* was in full stride, the collision caused her to loose her balance and crash to the ground. She slid for some distance before coming to a painful stop.

The matriarch threw her head forward. The exhausted hadrosaur, who had stopped running at the moment of impact, was unable to dodge the attack. The *Albertosaurus* jaws latched onto his neck, blade-like teeth penetrating deep into his flesh. The awesome power of the *carnivore's* jaws held fast.

The wild chase now became a frantic struggle. The female held the massive, thrashing animal by the neck, while the remainder of the pack caught up and circled the combatants. They were trying to grasp the flailing tail or the back of the herbivore's legs in order to eliminate its chances of escape. One of the circling pack was successful in avoiding the lashing tail of the hadrosaur, and with one of its powerfully clawed feet ripped open the leg of the doomed animal.

The animal's struggles became weaker and his head lowered toward the ground. The *Albertosaurus* held on for a few more minutes to be sure the fight was over. When she could feel no motion, she released her grip and allowed the animal to fall.

The victorious hunt leader walked around the kill while the rest of the pack stood back, agitated and obviously excited. The dominant male approached the female, roaring his approval and satisfaction with her hunting efforts. As a sign of affection he

grasped her head, putting his mouth around hers. The female, not expecting this gesture, jerked her head back. As she did, his teeth cut her flesh deeply along her mouth before he was able to open his mouth to release her. She roared her fury and snapped her jaws. The male retreated to the other members of the pack, obviously rebuked.

The sun slipped behind the clouds lying low on the western horizon. The large female settled down to feed on the fresh kill and the rest of the pack joined her. By the time the sun had set, the tyrannosaurs had finished their meal. The nine animals moved to the forest edge to find a suitable sleeping area.

_____

When morning broke, the pack moved slowly north along the trail. Their best chance for finding food at this time of year was to follow the large herds of migrating herbivores.

The dominant female led the way. Her position was supreme and every one of the pack members knew this. When one of the young bulls moved too close to the front of the pack, the matriarch snapped her jaws in displeasure. The younger animal retreated. At some time in the future her dominance would be challenged by the younger females in the pack. However, this was not going to happen today.

A strong north-westerly wind carried a familiar scent to the predators. With their noses raised to sniff the air, they traced the origin of the smell. Somewhere ahead was a close relative, *Daspletosaurus,* which was also a large tyrannosaur. It was a little bulkier than *Albertosaurus,* which gave it more success attacking heavily armed ceratopsid dinosaurs.

Being in the same area as *Daspletosaurus* was not safe for the *Albertosaurus.* They would not be in direct competition for food, but they were still in danger of being attacked by the larger animal. There was another scent in the air, fresh blood. The *Albertosaurus* matriarch forged ahead in the direction of the scent. A confrontation was inevitable as long as these beasts shared the same hunting ground, and she preferred to have that confrontation on her terms. After walking for a short time, the pack saw two *Daspletosaurus* drinking from a muddy pond. The approaching *Albertosaurus* pack spread out into a crescent, gesturing and roaring.

The *Daspletosaurus* quickly turned toward the approaching pack. The two groups of animals moved to within five body lengths of each other and stopped. The *Daspletosaurus* lowered their heads and let out shrieking bellows of anger at the intrusion into their territory. There was a partially devoured ceratopsian lying at the edge of the pond, and they did not want to leave it.

The sound was deafening as the enormous carnivores roared their anger at each other. The noise continued for a few minutes with no movement made by either group.

Suddenly, the largest of the *Daspletosaurus* leapt forward, snapping his jaws. This was a very brave or a very foolish gesture, considering he was facing nine fierce beasts that were almost as large as he. Taken off guard by the unexpected move, the central members of the pack retreated a few steps. The second *Daspletosaurus* joined the first.

After a moment's hesitation, the largest *Albertosaurus* male moved to within a body length of his foe. It was obvious the *Daspletosaurus* would not be intimidated by mere gestures. The *Albertosaurus* lunged forward and snapped at the nearest

Daspletosaurus. Two of his teeth grazed the side of the massive beast's head, leaving only slight cuts on the larger animal. The small right forearm of the *Daspletosaurus* lashed out at the attacker's right side, but his claws barely penetrated the thick leathery skin.

Moving back, both animals resumed their ritual of bellowing and jaw snapping. The rest of the pack moved closer to the confrontation. The two *Daspletosaurus* realised they were about to be overwhelmed by the sheer number of their opponents, and they backed up slowly to the carcass. The younger, faster *Albertosaurus* started to harass and badger their larger cousins, running in from behind to snap at the angrily twitching tails, and moving back as the enraged giants turned on them. It was clear that the only option for the *Daspletosaurus* was retreat. Turning suddenly, they passed through an opening the *Albertosaurus* had left in their circle. The *Albertosaurus* pack pursued them for a short distance, and then returned to finish off the carcass of the ceratopsian. There was no more than a mouthful of food for each, and the matriarch soon gestured for the pack to turn their attention towards the open plain.

As the nine pack members resumed their journey north, the dry ferns of the plains were crushed under their huge feet. It had not rained for nearly six weeks. By late afternoon, thunderheads could be seen towards the west. Within an hour, sporadic rain showers were sweeping across the plains in broad bands, and brilliant streaks of lightning were producing peal after peal of deafening thunderclaps. A tall *Albertosaurus* on the open plain was like a lightning rod, and the animals instinctively knew they were in danger. They moved towards the wooded margins of the foothills again.

Soon they passed into a coniferous forest that closed in and blocked their vision in all directions. The *Albertosaurus* meandered around trees that dwarfed them in height and girth. The ground surrounding these majestic trees had been trampled hard by the thousands of animals that had passed beneath their high branches.

Lack of rain was evident everywhere. The few young trees that had not been eaten by hadrosaurs snapped when the huge animals brushed against them. Claps of thunder rumbled above the forest canopy. But no rain reached the thick dry mat of needles and dead branches that littered the ground.

Evening was again upon the pack. They had travelled a long way today and each member was extremely tired. The matriarch looked for a suitable spot to spend the night. Even though the pack had eaten only lightly on the ceratopsian, they did not feel the need to eat before sleeping for the night.

Darkness found the *Albertosaurus* nestled between the trees. The last to fall asleep, the matriarch listened to the sound of nocturnal animals hunting for food. Insects and small mammals, the creatures of the night, scampered about. This was the only time the small animals felt safe from the reigning giants. The large female glanced one last time at the sleeping pack and slowly closed her eyes.

Just before dawn, the *Albertosaurus* woke up to an unfamiliar smell. Fumes were irritating their noses and eyes. Overnight, smoke had infiltrated the forest, carried along the game trails by gentle but persistent breezes.

As they stood up, each *Albertosaurus* shifted uncertainly. They relied heavily on their senses of sight and smell for survival. The *pungent* aroma of the smoke was masking all scents, and their eyes were watering. The huge carnivores milled around in confusion. A bright yellow glow could be seen through the trees to the west, and there was a strange crackling noise.

The anxious predators knew they were in danger, but they did not know what the danger was. Instinctively, they started to move north. The forest was unnaturally noisy with flocks of birds and *pterosaurs* flying overhead, squawking as they went. The grunting of other dinosaurs became more frequent. It seemed everyone was agitated. From around the trees, eight *Struthiomimus* darted through the pack of *Albertosaurus.* The two species ignored each other. The danger they all sensed in the smoke-filled air overpowered the instincts of predator and prey.

The wind picked up, becoming warmer and stronger. The smoke was dense, and breathing became difficult. This put the pack into near frenzy. The matriarch started to run in an attempt to escape the unseen menace. The others followed. They all sensed that somehow this danger was different from any other they had encountered. Panic set in.

Moving through the trees, the matriarch could now see a bright orange glow. The pack was heading directly toward a wall of flames. The intense heat and roar forced the group to change directions. They veered east, their only hope of escape.

Racing through the forest, the pack came to a small hill leading down to a valley. Here the forest opened up into a large marsh, a possible refuge from the wall of flames following behind them. Smoke was quickly filling the valley and marsh.

The *Albertosaurus* came crashing out of the forest and into the marsh. Most of the beasts lost their footing as their great weight propelled them into the mud and water. Their momentum plunged them forward and four of the beasts fell and rolled, spraying mud and water into the air.

The *Albertosaurus* now faced a new enemy, the marsh. The combination of water, mud, vegetation and rotting logs made crossing the marsh a formidable task. Surging forward, every step took a huge amount of energy. Each foot sank deep into the mud and water. It took them a considerable amount of time to get near the centre of the marsh, and exhaustion was setting in.

The *Albertosaurus* stood still. Even though the smoke was becoming thicker and the wall of flames encroached on the marsh, they had to rest.

The matriarch felt the intense heat once again. Whirlwinds of smoke danced along the marsh's surface. This was enough to force the pack to move again. The mud was deeper in the middle of the marsh and the animals strained to heave their legs through the muck. Already two of the younger adults had become stuck. They could only watch as the giant figures of the pack faded away in the smoke.

The remaining animals struggled on through the marsh. They had no choice but to continue inhaling the deadly smoke. Gulping and gasping with each step, they fought for the oxygen they needed to go on. But one by one they fell, succumbing to the smoke that filled their lungs. Soon, only the large female was still alive. She looked back and could no longer see any of her once mighty pack.

A dizziness overpowered the matriarch. She had been the strongest of her pack and had successfully defeated many enemies. But all her power was useless against this final foe. Smoke filled her lungs and toxins flooded her body. With her last breath she let out a mighty shriek. She looked up at the deadly sky once more before all went dark and she toppled over on her side.

The main part of the fire passed around the marsh that day, burning the trees to the ground and igniting everything in its path. Most of the marsh remained untouched by the fire. A heavy layer of soot and ash covered everything, including nine silent forms stretched out in the mud and water.

Albertosaurus sarcophagus

Albertosaurus sarcophagus is one member of a small family of very successful meat-eating *(theropod)* dinosaurs that lived during Late Cretaceous times (between about 100 and 65 million years ago) in the Northern Hemisphere. Its remains have been found from Mexico in the south to Alaska in the north. Specimens from Mongolia and China identified as *Albertosaurus* are more likely a larger tyrannosaur known as *Tarbosaurus batar*. Two other well-known tyrannosaurs are *Gorgosaurus libratus* and *Tyrannosaurus rex.*

Authors Eric P. Felber and Philip J. Currie excavating skull of *Gorgosaurus*, close relative of *Albertosaurus*. (Photograph by Jan Sovak.)

When Joseph Burr Tyrrell of the Geological Survey of Canada led his first expedition to Alberta in 1884, he did not realise the wide-ranging consequences of his search for minerals. He and his assistants found coal in the valley of the Red Deer River, near the present-day city of Drumheller. But they also found something else. On June 9, 1884, the Tyrrell team discovered the first dinosaur bones ever recovered from the Alberta badlands. Today these badlands are considered one of the most important sources of dinosaur fossils in the world.

The fossils discovered that first day were nothing special. But a few weeks later, Tyrrell got a fright. He walked around a point of rock on a ledge halfway up a cliff and found the skull of a carnivorous dinosaur leering at him from its rocky grave. Using geological hammers and axes, they removed the skull and some other bones in an afternoon. They had no packing materials or crates, so the specimens were lowered gently to the bottom of the hill and put onto a wagon.

The delicate cargo was hauled slowly across the prairies to Calgary. The trip, which today takes less than an hour and a half by car, took a week. The specimen was eventually delivered safely to the vaults of the Geological Survey in Ottawa. In recent years, staff of the Royal Tyrrell Museum of Palaeontology have collected two more *Albertosaurus* skeletons only a few hundred yards from where J. B. Tyrrell found his specimen.

In 1884, the fossilised skull Tyrrell found was the best dinosaur evidence that had ever been discovered in Canada. Then, in June of 1889, another

Two inch *Albertosaurus* tooth was found in the cavity of a hadrosaur shoulder blade. (Photograph by Lawrence Dohy.)

Badlands near *Albertosaurus* bone bed. (Photograph by Eva Koppelhus.)

Geological Survey party, this time led by Thomas Chesmer Weston, discovered another *Albertosaurus* skull as they floated down the Red Deer River by boat.

The skulls found by Tyrrell and Weston were studied by some very distinguished palaeontologists. Edward Drinker Cope of Philadelphia examined them, and in 1898 determined that they belonged to *Laelaps incrassatus*. *Laelaps* was a dinosaur that he had named more than thirty years earlier on the basis of fossils from New Jersey. Unfortunately the name turned out to be invalid because it had been used previously for another type of animal.

In 1904, Lawrence Lambe of the Geological Survey classified the two skulls as being *Deinodon*, a genus based on teeth found in Montana half a century earlier. But this name also had difficulties. Several types of carnivorous dinosaurs have almost identical teeth, so it was difficult to determine whether or not the specimens from Alberta were the same animal as *Deinodon*.

Henry Fairfield Osborn finally proposed the name *Albertosaurus sarcophagus* in 1905, the year when Alberta became a province of Canada. At the same time he published his first descriptive paper on *Tyrannosaurus rex.*

In 1910, a field party from the American Museum of Natural History (New York) was floating down the Red Deer River, looking for dinosaur skeletons. The leader of this party was Barnum Brown, one of the most famous and most experienced dinosaur collectors of that era. Upstream from the present town of Drumheller, they made a remarkable discovery. It began with a few bones of a carnivorous dinosaur. By the end of the first day they were convinced that they had found a complete skeleton. A few days later, they realised that it was an accumulation of at least five skeletons of *Albertosaurus.*

Brown did not keep very good field notes, and he never published a paper on the find, so we cannot be sure how significant he thought the site was. Yet when I "rediscovered" the specimens in the collections of the American Museum in 1996, it was clear to me that Brown knew he had found the first evidence for packing behaviour in large carnivorous dinosaurs. Although he did not excavate any complete skeletons, he removed enough hind limbs to suggest that at least nine *Albertosaurus* individuals had died at the same time.

Albertosaurus foot claw. (Photograph by Lawrence Dohy.)

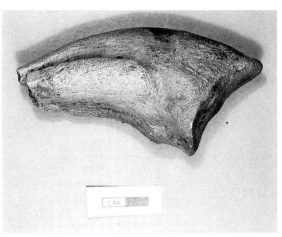

The fossils collected from the quarry showed that the animals ranged from four to nine meters (13 to 30 feet) in total length. All were found at the same level and were at the same stage of deterioration when they were buried. Other than two toe bones of a hadrosaur, no bones of other animals were found in the quarry. Because normally only one of every twenty dinosaurs found in the Drumheller region is *Albertosaurus,* domination by this animal in a single quarry is very powerful evidence that these animals were living together as a pack at the time of their deaths. The idea that some species of large meat-eaters travelled in packs is reinforced by a *Tyrannosaurus rex* quarry in which the remains of four individuals were found together. Also, there are several locations where carnivore trackways suggest that a number of animals were walking together.

Many other ideas presented in this story about *Albertosaurus* are also based on evidence found in the fossil record. More than half a dozen skeletons have been found that show injuries to the lower leg. Most of these consist of broken bones (*fibulae*) that subsequently healed. The height of the injury is often at about the level one would expect the club on a tail of an ankylosaur to hit if it tried to defend itself against a tyrannosaur. Ankylosaurs are often depicted as solitary animals. However, a number of sites in Asia, including one that we worked on in China, clearly show that they were gregarious, or social animals for at least some parts of the year.

Several incidents in the story emphasise the amazing power of tyrannosaur jaws, and the strength of their large, serrated teeth. There is a lot of evidence for this in the fossil record. The back half of a hadrosaur skeleton we excavated in 1977 near Drumheller was well articulated. This means that the bones were fairly complete and were lying almost in the right order. However, when we started to find isolated tyrannosaur

Albertosaurus teeth. (Photograph by Lawrence Dohy.)

Gorgosaurus quarry, Dinosaur Provincial Park. Fibula (leg bone) had been fractured and had healed. (Photograph by Eva Koppelhus.)

teeth mixed in with the ribs, we knew we were in trouble with the rest of the skeleton. As we worked our way forward through the rock, the skeleton suddenly turned into a mess of bone chips and tyrannosaur teeth. The entire front half of the hadrosaur, bones and all, had been eaten by one or more tyrannosaurs!

More recently, Greg Erickson and some colleagues from California conducted a very elaborate experiment. The hips of a *Triceratops* were discovered in Montana that had been chewed up by a *Tyrannosaurus rex*. There were deep puncture marks in the bones. The team measured the depth of the punctures, and manufactured some metal "tyrannosaur" teeth the size of the real ones that had made the punctures. The metal teeth were attached to a machine and were used to bite to the appropriate depth in modern cow bones. The amount of power necessary to drive the teeth into the bones was measured by the machine. Not surprisingly, they discovered that the power of a tyrannosaur jaw exceeds that of any living animal. This also explains why tyrannosaur teeth are so thickly built. Other theropod dinosaurs have thinner, more blade-like teeth. But tyrannosaur teeth were thick so that they could be used to bite into the bones of their prey without breaking. The muscles of the jaws also had to be strong enough to make this happen.

The fossil record has given us some clues that suggest the largest tyrannosaurs were in fact the females. Because female tyrannosaurs laid eggs as large as watermelons, they needed more room in the hip region. *Chevron bones* hang beneath the tails of most animals to protect the nerves and blood vessels, and to serve as attachment points for muscles. The first few tail vertebrae, at the base of the tail, often lack chevrons, however.

Badlands near Brown's 1910 *Albertosaurus* bone bed discovery. (Photograph by Eva Koppelhus.)

In tyrannosaurs, as in many modern reptiles, the female had one less chevron than the male. This effectively made the *pelvic canal* larger so that she could lay eggs. By counting the number of chevron bones, palaeontologists can distinguish between male and female tyrannosaurs. The largest tyrannosaur found to date is a specimen that the Black Hills Institute for Geological Research excavated and named "Sue". The specimen was named after its discoverer, Sue Hendrickson. The name turned out to be appropriate because it was a female *T. rex*.

At one point in the story, the matriarch of the pack is bitten on the face by one of the males. There is a lot of evidence to suggest that this may have been part of the courtship ritual of tyrannosaurs. A scientific paper done by Darren Tanke and myself suggests that the high incidence of bite marks on tyrannosaur jaws is similar to many modern animals (including fish, reptiles and mammals) in which face-biting is a normal part of their behaviour.

We have depicted *Albertosaurus* as a predator specialised to kill hadrosaurs. It was a lighter, faster animal than *Daspletosaurus*, but it lived at the same time in the same region. There is a weak correlation that shows *Albertosaurus* may have fed mostly on hadrosaurs, and *Daspletosaurus* may have preferred ceratopsians. For example, at sites where you find more ceratopsians, you will also find more *Daspletosaurus*. Towards the end of the Cretaceous, both *Albertosaurus* and *Daspletosaurus* disappear. Ceratopsian dinosaurs became very common after that, and not surprisingly it is *Tyrannosaurus rex*, the direct descendent of *Daspletosaurus*, that becomes the dominant predator.

Regardless of food preferences, all theropods were probably opportunists that scavenged when they found dead carcasses. However, the occasional dead carcass would not feed a pack of hungry *Albertosaurus* for very long. In contrast, the giant flying reptile *Quetzalcoatlus* weighed less that a German Shepherd dog, and with its efficient means of moving

Jaw and teeth of *Gorgosaurus*. (Photograph by Jan Sovak.)

great distances as a flier and glider, it may have been able to find sufficient food as a scavenger.

The organised nature depicted in tyrannosaur hunting behaviour in this book also has some basis in fact. A young tyrannosaur, such as those found in the *Albertosaurus* bone bed near Drumheller, had very long, slim legs in comparison with its body size. This means that they were capable of running very fast. That would have allowed them to keep up with the adults, which had longer legs overall but were much more heavily built. Because they travelled in packs, one can easily imagine that they divided up the labour in such a way that the younger, faster animals probably had a very different role to play than the larger, heavier adults.

The theme of migration is prevalent in this book. We know that large dinosaurs lived in Arctic regions during the Late Cretaceous, but suspect that it may have been for only part of the year. There is ample evidence that some species of hadrosaurs and ceratopsians moved in large herds at times. We suspect that they may have collected into these herds to move north into the polar regions during the summer months when there were 24 hours of sunlight every day. In the fall they would collect into herds again and move south to escape the prolonged darkness of winter, when food would have been difficult to find at such high latitudes.

The Royal Tyrrell Museum of Palaeontology will reopen Brown's *Albertosaurus* quarry in 1998 to collect more specimens, and to see if we can determine the cause of death of the nine *Albertosaurus.* One possible cause is forest fire. Animals that die thus do not usually show signs of the fire. However, burned wood can be preserved as charcoal in the fossil beds. It is something we will be looking for as we excavate more of the *Albertosaurus* bones. One thing we can be sure of, the circumstances must have been very unusual to have killed so many top predators. Regardless of what we learn, we feel that the fictional events portrayed in this story reflect our most up to date scientific understanding of what *Albertosaurus* may have been like in life.

J.B. Tyrrell's discovery of *Albertosaurus* skull.

GLOSSARY

adrenaline: a hormone produced by the body that stimulates the heart.

Albertosaurus: "Alberta lizard"; a type of meat-eating dinosaur related to *Tyrannosaurus rex*.; first discovered in 1884 near the present city of Drumheller, Alberta, Canada.

agitated: excited, disturbed.

ankylosaurs: slow moving, armoured dinosaurs; the tail of some species ended in a great knob of bone that was used as a defensive weapon.

carcass: a dead body.

carnivore: meat eater.

ceratopsian: "Horned faced" dinosaurs; plant-eating, bird-hipped dinosaurs that lived during the Late Cretaceous period, from about 100 until 65 million years ago; characterised by horns on the face and a frill that extends from the back of the skull over the neck.

chevron bones: small bones that hang beneath the tail to protect nerves and blood vessels.

conifer: evergreen trees (gymnosperms).

Cretaceous: the last period (approximately 100 million to 65 million years ago) of the Mesozoic era; marked by the greatest diversity of dinosaurs, a great increase in flowering plants, and the diversification of mammals; the period ends with the extinction of many types of animals, including all dinosaurs other than birds.

cycads: a gymnosperm (a seed plant in which the seeds are not enclosed in an ovary); looks like a palm but belongs to an entirely different order (Cycadales) which is the second largest order of living gymnosperms; today they grow in tropical and subtropical parts of the world.

Daspletosaurus: a bulky member of the tyrannosaur family.

demise: death.

foraging: wandering in search of food.

hadrosaur: duck-billed dinosaur; a group of plant-eating animals that were very successful at the end of the Cretaceous period.

herbivore: plant-eater.

matriarch: a female who rules or dominates a family or group.

migratory: to migrate is to move periodically from one region to another primarily for feeding purposes; the migratory route is the path followed.

parkland: areas of land that are covered by ground vegetation interspersed with stands of trees.

peril: danger, risk.

pelvic canal: passage from internal organs through the hips to the outside of the body for excretion, defecation, egg laying, etc.

predator: a meat eating animal that hunts its prey.

pterosaurs: flying reptiles that became extinct shortly before the end of the Cretaceous Period; distantly related to dinosaurs and birds.

pungent: causing a sharp or irritating sensation.

Quetzalcoatlus: largest known pterosaur; found in Alberta, Montana, Texas and Wyoming.

Saurornitholestes: close relative of *Velociraptor.*

serrated: notched edge of a saw or knife; a ridge on a tooth bearing tiny tooth-like projections.

Struthiomimus: one of the ostrich-mimic dinosaurs.

theropod: name given to all of the meat-eating dinosaurs.

tyrannosaur: the popularized name of a family that included some of the largest, and most sophisticated flesh-eating dinosaurs, *Tyrannosaurus rex*, *Albertosaurus*, *Daspletosaurus*, etc.